The Female Crisis

Chloe Rogers

BookLeaf Publishing
India | USA | UK

The Female Identity Crisis © 2023 Chloe Rogers

All rights reserved.

No part of this publication may be reproduced, stored in a retrieval system, or transmitted, in any form or by any means, electronic, mechanical, photocopying, recording or otherwise, without the prior written permission of the presenters.

Chloe Rogers asserts the moral right to be identified as author of this work.

Presentation by *BookLeaf Publishing*

Web: www.bookleafpub.com

E-mail: info@bookleafpub.com

ISBN: 9789358316162

First edition 2023

DEDICATION

This book is dedicated to Leo and Mabel, my cubs. You have my whole heart, forever and always

ACKNOWLEDGEMENT

I'm eternally grateful for my two children, Leo and Mabel, who have given me the greatest gift within a lifetime, in being their Mummy. It was the one role I confidently knew I always wanted to be, and they have provided me with more purpose and the deepest level of love humanly possible. Without them, I wouldn't have been able to feel or experience half of the content of this book. My two cubs, I hope one day you'll read this and understand. I hope this also shows you that you can always chase your dreams.

To my Russell- the man who showed me the deepest level of love I deserved. He came into my life at a time I was healing and searching for myself again. Without his support and encouragement, and without his incredible ability to truly see me, I would still be 'lost'. There are not enough words to express my gratefulness for the huge part you have played in my recovery and for demonstrating the qualities I need and adore in a life-partner.

I want to express a deep appreciation for my parents who have always loved and supported me during times it wasn't easy to. Though there were many repercussions and years of hurdles following their separation, it is only now that I have been able to fully see it from all angles. I understand they too were always learning and that the selfless commitment to your children lasts a lifetime.

PREFACE

Poetry has always felt like therapy to me, from my teen years as a bystander to my parents' divorce, to navigating the separation of my own relationship to the father of my two young children. But when it came to expressing my struggles in motherhood and the impact it has had on my wider purpose and goals in life, I held back from the judgement of my own words.

It became inherently obvious that this collection of poetry deserved its place to be heard by other women who perhaps are harnessing similar paradoxical thoughts. After one too many grenades being flown from, or towards my direction as I approached my thirties with an abandoned career, flailing relationships and ill-health, I poured my deepest and sometimes darkest emotions into this book.

Whether it can be viewed as a rehabilitation, recovery or reflection on your own self, I invite you to explore the great challenges and equally rewarding elements of finding your place in this modern world as a woman.

Glory Script

Remember when you were small,
When the judgement of others didn't phase you at all
When you'd simply live for the moment you're in,
And you wouldn't battle the voice within
You'd pick up a pen and draw happy faces,
And look for love in all the right places
Life was fulfilled from the simplest of things
No self-imposed deadlines or pressure time brings
Take a page from your younger self's book,
Revisit the chapters of how your life looked
Did you think of the consequence when you drew on the wall?
Did you worry what other's thought at all?
You learned as you went from script to script,
Left the drafts in the past and became more equipped,
To turn the next page with pride and glory,
Treat today as the same, and write your own story

Little Universe

I hold you like you're all my soul has been searching for,
and the warmth of your skin radiates mine
I wonder- were we connected in a previous life?
Because I instantly feel glad to have you home

The magic that happens with your face against mine,
It instantly eases us both, and my pounding heart slows
I marvel in amazement- do you feel the energy too?
Because it's beyond a physical realm I've known

You gaze at me in wonder and deep ocean eyes
Beyond my reflex smile, I see right into you
I pour my love over you- do you feel this is where you belong?
Because I do, without having known you at all

The Mother in Me

Woven into my veins beyond my existence
An intrinsic love that's become my being
A light so bright, that's sometimes blinding
Connection that fibres my soul into theirs
They are me, and I have become them
Every thought of my own has a shadow
A reflex response for the people I carried
I will never be the same again

Selfless Love

Love you hard, love you deep, love forever to keep
Love you day, love you night, love you blind and in sight
Love you right, love you wrong, love you where you belong
Love you near, love you far, love wherever you are
Love your skin, love your bones, love you're never alone

Skin

'Love the skin you're in', they say,
but what if the best 'you' was back in the day?
When lashes and nails and tanning beds,
Gym-days, counting-syns-days filled the week ahead
Diets, prepped lunches and protein shakes,
Bought a blender for soups and smoothies to make
When all of my hours and pounds were spent,
On the hair and self-care for the selfies I sent

But it wasn't vanity in case you should say,
Loving myself never came into play
With a flat tummy, thin pins, I'd still try to hide,
My body on holiday and the 'me' inside
How could it be I sought so much approval?
No wonder it crushed me when I had some refusals
My identity was for others to define
Brains and books, pinned it all on my looks,
The voice of doubt so loud all the time

Now my opinion has more volume
Trust and value it more than I used to
I know who I am and I know where I'm going

Stand up tall, love it all, even while I'm still growing
To be as 'big' as I thought I was then,
My best physical version way back when,
I'd spend money and time on my body,
Now I'm focused on other priorities
When loving the skin you're in used to mean,
Gymming and swimming and eating clean
Other parts of me to know and to love
I'm me, I'm not changing for all the above

Heavy Load

I'm fighting, slipping backwards,
Clinging on with white finger tips
I'm heavy, I'm slow,
While you rest on my aching hips

I'm balancing the load,
It's a universe I've chosen
I bare weight in my arms,
Take a seat on my shoulders

I lose my breath,
I'm strong but feel weak,
I can't hear my voice,
But for you I'll still speak

I moved mountains inside,
To make way for your growth
A pocket to protect you,
So you could walk this earth

Lost

Lost and confused, for which way to choose,
searching for something unknown
My heart longs and aches for scenes my head makes,
For lust in my dreams that I'm shown

Chasing memories and all that's behind me,
for a feeling I had once before
Replay and repeat, the times that we'd meet,
I sit in its comfort once more

To the future I look, a whole new book,
changing the chapters I'd written
I'm alive and on fire, in danger, desire,
Chewing easily all I had bitten

Then I'm back to the now, fearful somehow,
Of these visions that keep on coming
Does it mean that I'm lost, to risk at all costs,
The security blanket I'm wrapped in

Cocooned and still, contentment is real,
For the life we have carved in the woods
Where we're shadowed, protected, the light is deflected,

Sheltered from where we are stood

Lost and still searching, something I'm unearthing,
Below the sturdy roots where I'd grown
The more thoughts get watered, the more that I'm tortured,
or nurtured by what I don't know

Battle Scars

Been in the trenches for months if not years,
Defending my land and my tribe
Shielded in armour and under attack,
Searching for ways to survive

There were mornings of hope and new days ahead,
Phases of loving deep
Under the moon in a purple dark haze,
Treasuring moments to keep

Just as the stillness and peace had set in,
We relaxed and let down our guard
Gunshots were fired, crash and spit,
Now bullets are raining down hard

Let Me Be

Let my heart be numb,
For I wish not to feel hardship anymore

Let my heart be cold,
For I wish not to feel the depths of disappointment

Let my heart be still,
For I wish not to feel it pull in different directions

Let my heart be rested,
For I wish not to feel it race against time

Let my heart be light,
For I wish not to feel it's crushing weight

Let my heart be-
For I wish not to try and fight, nor argue with it anymore

For the Kids

We stay and we fight- let's battle it out!
Too many days where we scream and shout
How about we call it a day?
But it's never made final, and we don't seem to mind to,
Sweep all the problems away

So much silence, too loud to ignore,
Just can't be bothered to talk anymore
How about we shut the door?
And then when it's time, to say our goodbyes,
We find reasons to stay once more

Not enough cuddles, kisses or cares,
Selfish in ways that's just not fair
How about we say 'that's enough'?
I find a track, stay strong, turn my back,
But the pull is way too tough

I sink and you swim; you lose and I win,
competition we always live within,
How about we end it all?
I beg, 'let me go', will myself to say no,
The pattern repeats and in it we fall

Not much left, not even sharing a bed,
I dream of days that are brighter ahead
When do we say goodbye?
In my head I'm gone, now the guilt is strong
Now I'm truly living a lie

30 Seconds

The anxiety is rising, It's a matter of seconds,
Before I must pause- my thought process and errands
Another need, another want or demand;
A call for my attention or helping hand;
A story to decipher, an argument to resolve;
Clothes change, toilet runs, play-doh to mould;
Nose-wipes, shoes to put on, faces to clean;
Snacks to open, juice top-ups in between;
Emotions to nurture, stimulation to give;
Read the books, play with toys, find the pens to colour with;
Answer questions, surf through kids TV;
Syringe calpol, apply plasters, and then leave them be;
Race back to the kitchen, start dinner prep just when,
I have 30 seconds before I'm needed again

Biding Time

The hourglass that keeps on giving,
The weeds that keep on living
When does the curtain fall?
'You done your best, take a seat and rest'
Are words I can't fathom at all

The second-hand flies while the hour hand creeps by,
A fast and slow juxtaposition
What do I wait for, why do I stay more?
When I've already made my decision?

A stony old sun dial with flaking paint,
It still tells the time, no matter how faint
Dying and constantly living
I've no fire inside, no batteries alive
Why do I keep on giving?

The world that keeps on turning,
The stars that keen on burning,
The telescope that forever sees
Capturing its glow and yet it's unknown,
When the light went out exactly

'There is no right time',

means you can't get it wrong, right?
Just leap and hope you land
When you're biding the minutes,
for what you're not sure,
Just trust you got this in hand

Broken Home

I'm sorry I couldn't love you in the right way,
And that I've run out of road to make me stay
I wanted the pieces of us to stay glued,
So I've hung on for longer than I knew I should do
Look through the windows and see the pain,
Leave your pride at the door, wash your words down the drain
The ceiling, once without limit, is falling heavy,
Like my heart that drops and staggers unsteady
The gutters are caving in weight of tears,
While we stand there drowning in thoughts and fears
The foundations are breaking beneath our feet,
Gaping holes, deep and vast beneath the concrete
The writing is there to see on the walls,
Shredded remnants from papering over it all
Now tell me you can't see the dimming lights?
Tired and lacking in fire and fight
Alarms are ringing angry, persistent
But you cover your ears, so boldly ignorant
Brick by brick, we built it all
In dust and debris, down it falls
Exit signs blindly illuminate,

the ways to escape before we suffocate
But we stay, ride it out, shut it down, let's forget?
Shield ourselves from the roof that was meant to protect
When do we leave, see the signs, save ourselves?
Now it's a blackout so in darkness we delve
Clinging onto the pieces that we call home
Parallel, but separate, in the corridors alone
Feeling around for the way to the light
Which doorway to choose, desperately searching
Shattered glass, tricking and changing,
We brush past each other at different times,
We dip and we fall and we pull and we climb
Until we have made it: we're out. And alive.
Broken, and searching for a new place to thrive

Help

'I'm drowning' were the words I said,
Over and over again
You chose to see the intermittent smiles
Did you hear- I'm drowning?

'I'm struggling to cope', a phrase I spoke
So difficult to say
You see me surviving and getting by
Did you forget you saw me crying?

'I don't know where to turn', I begged
Desperate for guidance
I see you have loaded shoulders of your own
Did I mention- I can't find a way out?

'You weren't there, I needed you', I scream
Frantic and spiralling downwards
Now you're sat up, angry at my tone
Did I lose you too?

Change

You want the kite to fly higher,
while holding it back by the string
You want to feel light and weightless,
while gravity pulls you back in
Forever an eye on the stars,
with both feet firm on the ground
Dream of being a hero,
while tucked in your bed safe and sound

Take risk, embrace change,
Instead of sitting and wishing
Run head first into the waves,
To find what's been missing

Bucket List

I want...

To live out the simplest of moments in life,
Make adventures of them too
Camp under stars and sleep in the car,
And to feel all shiny and new

To swim in a lake on a hot summer's day,
Road trips with nowhere to go
Capture moments in time of pure happiness,
Not having to put on a show

To ride a horse along the sand,
And belly laugh with someone out loud
No money to spare, just good company
A heaven beneath the clouds

To write a book I'd share with the world,
To sing and perform on a stage
To walk down the aisle on the arm of my Dad,
To a love that would never age

To lie beneath the Northern Lights,
Take my children to see the world
Dance in the garden surrounded by friends

With my favourite boy and girl

To have all the fun doing nothing extreme.
Romance and to kiss in the rain
Fall head over heels and be swept off my feet
Over and over again

Lift Me Up

The door opens, into it's chamber you step
It has you now
You know it's bright out there, but you're
floating in a portal,
Of temporary darkness
It's time to decide your direction, your chosen
destination
You need to find it now
You're not sure where to head, you can't put
your finger on it
You're lost,
But worse: still
Nowhere to run, nowhere to hide, you're truly
stuck
You can't move
You lose air
You lose light
The outside world is waiting, for you to reappear
You're locked in
Flight and Fight
You ring the alarm
They don't know how to reach you
The noise and darkness grows louder, ringing in
your ears
Nobody comes to save you

You're desperate for someone on the outside, where it's bright
To choose your fate, press the button, pull you in
You don't want to be swallowed, lower than here
Lift me up
You don't want to step out, back where you started
Lift me up
Pull, and climb, and claw, and fight
Lift me up
Light, and air, and freedom draws closer
Lift me up
The alarms are less angry, it feels brighter, you can see
Lift me up
There's a face, in the mirror, staring back at you
Lift me up
You're panic is easing, you're searching and finding,
Lift me up,
Without realising, you've been moving all along
Lift me up,
The door opens, and out you step
You were all that you needed

Recovery

Out in the depths of the deep dark blue, you see me, I see you,
Floating on an ocean unknown
Back on the shore, hear the chaos call-
A distant and numbing tone

In vulnerable territory, can't see ahead of me,
Wave surges come and go
There's peace in the air, I'm weightless to bear,
Kicking at pace from below

I dip and you dive, we gasp and we thrive,
Holding on, limb to limb
Survival mode on, alone in the sun
Side by side we swim

Safe at last, held in your arms
The horizon just in view
My anchor, my guide, the support by my side
Lost as one in the blissful blue

Rubber Band

You can stretch me, bend me and tie me in knots,
My love for you will never be lost
Wherever I go I'll bounce right back,
Embrace you and squeeze you until time has lost track
You can test me and send me to full blown expansion
I'm fit to burst with love against tension
You've shaped me and made me a different form,
Flexed and unbreakable from the day you were born

Sorry

It's a word, it's a phrase, it's a statement of truth,
It's something that's said, but lives in it's proof,
Regret and guilt disguised behind pride,
An action to make while you set that aside

When you throw everything up in the air and try,
To survive, find your feet, into new life you dive
You've carried the weight of the world and then some,
Can't juggle again, or the work comes undone

To those I abandoned and left behind,
Can't fight for the 'fit', I'm sorry, I tried
It's the lightest I've felt and I can't risk to lose,
For so long, we've walked in too different shoes

To those I ignored then came back to life,
It's been there between us, cut the air with a knife
I'm sorry that it took me so very long,
A new 'me', and strength, I rebuilt while gone

To the children and man whose family I broke,
I promise I fought hard through fire and smoke,
The night I cracked, lost all my sanity,

Was the product of holding on too tightly

To myself, I'm sorry I ignored and didn't hear,
The depth of struggle, the fight and the fear,
To allow yourself the permission to breathe,
Instinctive motherhood truly took over me

Next Chapter

Shall we write our own story?
Close the rule book, throw it in the fire?
Stand back, watch the embers dance and then we can admire,
The fact we've jumbled the pages,
Changed the order of the chapters
We come at this with experience and a history already captured
It keeps me on the edge of my seat,
Excited for whatever comes next
A whole load of pictures before us but what matters is the text
The way our stories have begun,
They meet in the middle right here
Don't need anyone else to read or understand it because its clear-

You plus me make magic,
wouldn't have it any other way
Place it proudly on the shelf,
To be continued every day

Milton Keynes UK
Ingram Content Group UK Ltd.
UKHW020917300424
441987UK00015B/728

9 789358 316162